AF265323

Small Journeys

Poems 2009 - 2019

Karen West

For the angel who carried me

KAREN WEST

Table of Contents

Small Journeys

These are the small journeys that we take; these
minute, courageous forays on a stony path, in the dark,
alone and in the humble caretaking of the
scurrying creatures which cross the parched earth at our feet,
and the tiny, inexplicable stars above,
a trail of silver words tracking us over night's page.

And each love, too, is its own thing, each meeting and parting
a new journey in a different land. We carry with us the small
mementos of our travels; poems, a tin cup, opal earrings the colour of
sky. They haunt us, even while they keep us, like talismans,
from straying into the wild, where nothing grows
but bitter herbs, casting roots uselessly
into a dusty earth.

Surely to forgive is as transformative a power
as ever there was; I remember an angry man turned
to talking of the moon, the bend and toss of toi toi spears against
a hard wind, a Wellington night I cannot recall
without weeping, but also without malice.

We bend to these aches, grass to wind, but we carry them
with tender delicate fingers, keepsakes against the cold.
On the rough path under the stars, I plod still,
the weight of the past soothing against my back.

And then, only the stars are left to navigate me on,
wakeful and still points of light, signposts in a new land.
The scurrying night creatures having disappeared
long ago, I am left only with a fistful of dry earth, in which
a tiny bud of something green still
impossibly clings.

First Flight
(For B)

Above the clouds, the bluest day
in Antarctica, glaciers of cloud.
The mountains gleam against a
splendiferous wing-stretch of blue.

First flight, take-off was breathless,
wordless wonder. Somewhere,
you are below. You slip between my fingers
like fine snow.

This morning early, I held you tight.
Now, a thousand clouds up,
the air is exquisitely light.

I contemplate the absurd; Amundsen, traversing an
impossible landscape, Scott's heroic failure,
you, down there squinting, looking up for a sign;
a drop of snow on your summer's day, a tiny flag
planted in the clouds.

I open a window,
casually step out onto the white,
cotton-wool solidity of this landscape,
allow my fingers to trail over the cloud-snow.
As a sign, I drop my pen into the
milk-white landscape below my feet,
watch it break through, free falling,
turning over slowly in the wind.

Pirongia '75

As children we used to run wild
the farm, an arrogant possession of
woolsheds, warmer days.
Giggle-streamed, a seamed and rolling land was
the garden of all our childish imaginings.
The brilliant yellow flare of gorse and
long days, hot as the creek was cold,
fallen trees a ride of splendid horses;
these are the constants
of dusty child-adventurers.

And always at our faces, the mountain;
looming and dark,
bringer of lean, cracking storms,
the rising river's flood, and
that strange, unearthly light, casting itself wildly,
like a lame hawk, against our
open-mouthed faces.
The misted, angular peaks always
beckoned us upward though we didn't dare,
those Patupiarehe slyly waiting
in the silent, wet undergrowth.
Then, we hid in safety behind rain-streamed windows,
cinnamon-bread-scented air.

The dusty roads of paddock-hot days
trail into the past; those grey mists which hung
over the mountain have dried up,
gone with a distant echo of thunder.
And the light that reeled and shied with the wind into the mountain's
great face is complacent at last.

The magic is worn out, along with the little people,
tired of waiting. All there is left is a dog,
barking voicelessly
into a thin wind.

Invocation to Black and White

What prayer is this?
Now I lay me down to sleep
upon the white cool sheets,
bare to line verse and meter,
a worn heart's rhythm.
I shuffle words like a small
blind creature; scrabble chips on a
stretching rack for dry bones.

I ask only for my soul's keeping,
and a pen that goes.
But words are lost in the ink, unbirthed.
The still white page covers them
as quickly as I can get them down.

Poem curls around my pen, scratching
the earth of things like
a snuffling animal
nosing blindly the inky night.

I touch him wonderingly,
watch as he curls into a small,
indigo ball, like a full stop
on a blank page.

On the Threshold

On the eve of my forty-third birthday
it is twilight, and I,
I am a small aching thing.
you having gone, a bad text,
Van Morrison moving like light through the air.
'I am standing on the threshold,
I am standing at the door'
and suddenly you appear
rock up, push bike and all, at my door

and where I was, *'I am not in love, but*
I'm open to persuasion'; suddenly, you are here,
like some rough, beautiful, twilight magic
and I step over the threshold
like a sigh, free-falling on the night.

Tonight, my birthday,
you gift me magic in a stone,
all twilight and phosphorescence,
beautiful thing.

Sheep's Dreams

Late in the night, a full moon glancing off the wolven dark,
you gone a grim hour, I lie under the humid hand of night,
hunted; I know the wolf in sheep's dreams.

For your birthday I gave you a knife. How many ways
can you cut me? Long ago I took that stony path in courage, in
moon's dark; now feel the full weight of fear each time I wake.

We began in reflected light, borrowed luminescence.
I did not consider the planting cycles, but forged ahead, light-struck and
blind, the moon painting us awake, eyes closed, with phantom daylight.

Now dreams thicken and turn as I open my eyes,
fall down upon to me upon my woken eyes, a burden of darkness.
And you come here, and leave, and I sleep again,

moving ahead of the pursuit of some nameless shape.
Oh, how not to bear the sharpness of the pain!
And as if moonlight stuck the dream harshly,

I blink in surprise, call your name.
I have come full circle, full moon again.

Running Poem

This is the country I travel,
the landscape of my running;
angular, twilight shadows
and darkness, tarmac and concrete,
the sound of my heartbeat.

A runner's life is a lonely life,
the road a dream under
gathering night.
Tarmac and concrete,
my heartbeat.

Is the pounding in my ears my
heart's exhausted rush or
my feet hitting the ground
in perpetual motion?

Sometimes I find myself drifting between
sky and road, neither one nor the other.
The rhythm of my breathing rasps
unbearably.

To move forward is all I can do,
falling, flying, dreaming,
tarmac and concrete,
the sound of my heartbeat.

Coming Home

It's funny how we come, eventually
to seek out our roots, to come home to the
warmth of the familiar; as if to enter a new decade
we must search out and greet again, other lost ones,
these children we left behind, but who now come to guide us
like gentle signposts, back home.

So this morning I find I am
traversing the length of my life in a landscape.
Travelling south fast, away from the city,
into a mist of greens and greys and shards
of memories, I look for signs.

Behind the mist, the hills are only subtle shapes in a
dreamful land, impressions in
an obscured vision slanted
with rain and *toi toi* spears.
Somewhere, hiding beneath the rocks,
memories with familiar eyes blink and hold, watch
me pass by, remembering.

The landscape of my life, too, has subtly
become obscured; I am lost in a mist
with nothing but the map of my heart;
but the shape of the land remains unaltered,
leads me, like a lighthouse,
back home.

American Dreaming

I belong in the northern hemisphere
where I dream I sit in
sun-riddled June days,
and earth's tilt rocks me into a
comfortable slouch, where I can
read the dozy afternoon away.

I belong in the northern hemisphere
where March and April thaw the
icy New York streets, and May gives way
to spring and summer,
summer solstice June,
hot, buzzy, delicious July
and August, God, we had eighty-five today,
I'd say complacently, stirring my iced lime.

Fall in New England, an October of orange,
reds and yellows, All Hallows Eve and ripe fruit
hailing the hidden Holly King
and a New York February, white Yule.

Instead I'm stuck here, on the
upside down of the world
like the hanged man,
dizzy and disorientated,
the seasons all in the wrong places,
the calendar year an absurd procession of events as if
the gods got confused, so just randomly
joined them end to end,
hoping they got it right,
or the seasons themselves switched places like
naughty brothers, to see if anyone
will notice.

Playing With Fire

Out of the late spring evening, you lit
the doorway like a candle.
A grey moth's heart fluttered.

You offer her light and warmth.
Will she singe her wings in the hot,
beautiful flame? Perhaps she'll burn
quickly, ash and bones
in a bruised darkness.

She follows you into the night,
taking her chances with fire in slow,
silver wing-beats. Later spirals down into
dawn's unearthly light,
fray-edged wings quivering.

Waiting

Each day is a mountain, heavy, unyielding,
infinitely slow. I strain against the hours like
a small bird, wings battered and frail,
heaving irrelevantly at the slow, immoveable arc of time.
The hours remain, empty, silent.

Today is the first cool day since summer, but I am
chill and hollow; my bones chink and scrape in
my body, settling into uneasy patterns of endless waiting.
In my stomach there is a stone.

The air is a thin skin stretched out over the afternoon.
Crows shock the air with harsh staccato,
taunting the endless stillness.
Yesterday your face turned to me in blank contemplation; I wanted
to reach out through the glass between us, but
you weren't there.

Another evening crawls out of the hills to lie
like a great, dark bird, over the world.
My breath stops in my throat.
Come home.

Wellington, New Year's Eve I

The city meets us with brittle, dark wind,
flying its inevitable welcome flag of pohutukawas,
spiny matagouri and nodding toi toi in cheerful, chill greeting.
It is the last day of December.

We have come winged on love's promise,
now stand entwined in the
city's light, waiting breathlessly for
the band to start, the music to roll
us forever into a memory, tightly.

And it does, with nine hundred others,
tucked onto the hillside and into the night.
The dark is a cocoon against the outside world;
we sleep, awake, in its safety.

The softness of your blue jumper against
my cheek makes my eyes inexplicably wet;
I hunker down into your warmth.
Fireworks carry us across time, to another year,
winking us on into a chilly January dawn.

The next day I depart, leaving you briefly,
a little rip to the skin of the heart
as you wave me off; matagouri and
gorse scramble for purchase on the rocks,
the ragged hillsides whispering in the wind
something I cannot hear.

Sums

They say at eleven weeks the pain recedes, but
to truly calculate the days until you might relax your
white-knuckled grip on the edge of each hard day
you must calculate the time you were coupled and
divide it precisely by half.
One hundred and thirty weeks divided by
lumps of my bloody, torn heart
equals precisely sixty-five weeks minus
the time already passed holding on to the last breath
I took before you left and holding it still,
which is seven weeks, and sixty-five weeks
minus that comes to fifty-eight weeks
to go and losing you is like having a limb
amputated with no anaesthetic.

Three weeks and thirteen months
to go, then, but the smaller, more incalculable
problems perplex me. There is no algorithm
for this: a shadow of you sits,
musing, on my blue couch; next
to you, the shape of a girl, weeping.

What You Brought
(For T)

All night long the dogs howl,
fill this winter of my sleeping.
I have lain awake forever, watchful, waiting,
under the vast press of night.
I falter under its weight, heaving helplessly.
This is an ancient, faithful creature;
its tail wags complacently, blackly encouraging.

Today, you came.
You brought with you a smattering of possessions,
some old photographs, your boots, an angel or two:
the detritus of a vagabond life; a caravan, you said with a smile.
I already know you brought more than just that.

Now, I lie awake again, and it pleases me to
imagine you, in the next room, doing
whatever vagabonds do – calmly sorting the impedimenta
of your life, or reading by lamplight, perhaps.
Whatever it is, you are only a wall away.
The great, grim howling of the dogs
is quieted. I sleep,
for the first time in weeks,
wake to the light.

Liminality

I stand in a strange, twilight land between
two countries; this nameless, liminal space, which sits between
the achingly familiar, and the terrible, indefinable newness
of things.

From my east-facing bedroom window, the moon hangs
on a background of inky night but
from my west windows, a pale sky crouches silently,
backlit with ghosts. I can touch neither,
so stand, unbreathing, in the center of it all.

I am jarred with the sudden displacement;
reality drifts like birds on a glass sky, and I drift
too, lifted out of my substance, to hover strangely over
an unrecognizable landscape.

Familiar objects anchor me fleetingly to this strange,
spinning world; my car, my red converse sneakers,
a favourite mug; they are the small constants which carry the
load of my life.

I am dizzy from holding on.
Face down on the ground, I cling to the hard earth,
for fear of lifting off, drifting into the nothing.

Wellington, New Years Eve II

It is too much, now, to come here.
The city's stark light strikes hard, over the tall buildings,
slices sharply the chill air. I breathe in; it sticks tightly
in my throat. Rain gathers over the city.
I ache, unrelentingly.

The nor'westerly coming into the
bus station batters the flesh and bone
of my grief, until I cannot bear it.
Everything is a memory, tightening
its hold.

From the bus, I look out over familiar landmarks: the viaduct, the
knoll of a grassy hill where we sat hunched into
the last of the year, dying in the light of the fireworks,
the café where we sat and ate salmon.

And the rocky hills, thick-scrubbed and angular with gorse,
sharp and unrelenting. I remember
voices and you, your blue jumper, the two of us squashed,
laughing, in a narrow bed,
in a room with no light.

I let the bus carry me away from it all,
up the Kapiti Coast, where you, last year, had come behind me;
I imagine you, on that bus, all you would have passed as I do now:
Pukerua Bay, Paraparaumu, paddocks a green blur, some marae
holding a Tangi in the rain, and then
over the startling hill where the huge wind machines
stand, endlessly flailing their arms at the great, grey sky.

Later I stand under the night, a country between us,
between the boundary of these two years.
I cannot move.
All I can do is look up,
eyes streaming in the stars' chill light.

Moving On

I quiver at the touch of the steel,
as cold and precise as the cuts
you make, as you carefully scissor
around my silhouette,
waiting for me to make a little cry, or gasp
as you graze my skin with the blades.
I relax my steely grip, let my hands drop uselessly
from the razor-sharp edge of the paper.
I am untethered now, loose, wandering on
the page of us.
Once my cut-out is done,
you discard me into the bin,
and there is left only a strange, empty me-shaped hole
I once inhabited.

I Did Not Expect Angels

I did not expect angels to
come trumpeting, over a high soft breeze and that
jaunty posturing five o'clock light, to settle
like dust particles, fine and transparent,
on the leaves of the palm trees which sway outside;
to watch intently my house as I came and went,
to hand me over the raging river in safety,
to beckon me off the busy road, nor when I cried, to taste
the salt of my tears off their fingers, wide-eyed.

No, I did not expect angels, in their myriads,
millions of white creatures fanning their
pure plumage in the sun as they sat on my roof quietly,
so as not to disturb with angel foot-fall,
keeping sentry over the doors and windows,
watching me sleep, then wake, then sleep again,
making sure my cat was fed and I turned
off the gas.

So when merely one knocked at my front door,
silver-haired, tattoos for skin, rosary hung at an
odd, rakish angle, his soft white wings
discretely folded and tucked into his battered sports bag,
and he asked me for a room,
you can imagine how I stared
in open-mouthed wonder.

Other poetry collections by Karen West

Between Is and Was

About the Author

Karen West is a native-born New Zealander, now living in Australia. Her second collection of poems looks towards ideas of memory, sentimentality, personal loss, and the resilience of human nature to move forward.

Contact Ms West at quantumgirl65@gmail.com